Diamond T 4-ton Truck

Written by David Doyle

Walk Around®

00807635

'Ole Bob'

479 AMPH. TRUCK CO.

1ST ENG. SPEC. BRIGADE

Squadron Signal Publications

Cover Art by Don Greer

(Front Cover) In something of a testament of to the robust construction of the 4-ton Diamond T, men of the 734th Ordnance Battalion, 7th Army, use their closed-cab wrecker to remove a Panzer IV from a French battlefield.

(Back Cover) An open cab 4-ton Diamond T belonging to the 969th Artillery Battalion serves as an artillery prime mover near Bastogne, Belgium, in December 1944.

About the Walk Around® Series

The Walk Around® series is about the details of specific military equipment using color and black-and-white archival and photographs of in-service, preserved, and restored equipment. *Walk Around*® titles are devoted to aircraft and military vehicles. These are picture books focus on operational equipment, not one-off or experimental subjects.

Squadron/Signal Walk Around® books feature the best surviving and restored historic aircraft and vehicles. Inevitably, the requirements of preservation, restoration, exhibit, and continued use may affect these examples in some details of paint and equipment. Authors strive to highlight any feature that departs from original specifications.

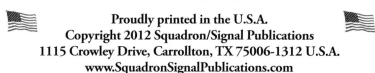

Proudly printed in the U.S.A.
Copyright 2012 Squadron/Signal Publications
1115 Crowley Drive, Carrollton, TX 75006-1312 U.S.A.
www.SquadronSignalPublications.com

Hardcover ISBN 978-0-89747-709-3
Softcover ISBN 978-0-89747-710-9

Military/Combat Photographs and Snapshots

If you have any photos of aircraft, armor, soldiers, or ships of any nation, particularly wartime snapshots, please share them with us and help make Squadron/Signal's books all the more interesting and complete in the future. Any photograph sent to us will be copied and returned. Electronic images are preferred. The donor will be fully credited for any photos used. Please send them to the address above.

(Title Page) The versatile and highly successful Diamond T 4-ton trucks served as prime movers, troop and cargo carriers, dump trucks, and wreckers. (James Alexander)

Acknowledgments

It would have been impossible to have created this book without the help of my friends. The late Kevin Kronlund provided unfettered access to an amazing collection of vehicles assembled by him and his wife Thea, including no fewer than four of the trucks shown in this book. Steve Greenberg and Joe Garbarino also generously provided access to their vehicles and responded to many queries. No less important was the extraordinary help of Tom Kailbourn, John Adams-Graf, James Alexander, Steve Preston, Chris Hughes, Pat Ware, and the late Fred Crismon. My wonderful wife Denise patiently traveled with me on multiple trips to several states as we researched this volume. As always, the professional staff at Squadron-Signal Publications went the extra mile to make the most of the materials I provided.

Introduction

Originally developed to fulfill the Quartermaster Corps' need for a prime mover for the 155mm howitzer, the WWII-era four-ton Diamond T truck boasted robust construction and a powerful Hercules engine. The Corps of Engineers found the truck to be well-suited for their needs, in particular as a dump truck, and strongly favored the Diamond T over the ubiquitous 2½ ton GMC CCKW cargo-dump. Unfortunately, the Diamond T cost twice as much as the CCKW, a considerable hindrance to mass procurement.

In addition to the short wheel base prime movers and dump trucks, a long wheel base version of the Diamond T was built for use by Canadian forces, and the widely used Diamond T 4-ton wrecker shared the short wheelbase chassis. Serving as the U.S. Army's standard medium wrecker during WWII and after, the Diamond T featured a twin-boom wrecker bed produced by Chattanooga's Ernest Holmes Company. The twin boom design allows side recoveries to be made by swinging one boom to that side, and swinging and tying off the other boom to the opposite side to stabilize the wrecker. For less severe loads, there were also stabilizer legs mounted on each side of the bed, just behind the cab. Typical of U.S. military wreckers, these trucks carried a wide array of recovery equipment, including chains, ropes, snatch blocks, cutting torches and tools, and even a gasoline-powered air compressor.

Although its U.S. military service life was just slightly over a decade, the Diamond T cast a long shadow and is generally recognized as the standard that the U.S. Army sought to achieve during the post-WWII development of tactical vehicles, including the M34/M35 series 2½ ton trucks and M41/M54 series five-ton trucks.

The Model 972 was the dump truck version of the 4-ton Diamond T. This early-production example, photographed in May 1944, had a soft cab and lacked a winch, which was present on later dump trucks as well as on all other Diamond Ts. (TACOM LCMC History Office)

Unlike the later production versions of the Diamond T cargo truck shown throughout the rest of the book, the earliest model, the Model 967, had a single brush guard assembly for the grille as well as the headlights. (Fred Crismon collection)

While strongly resembling a standard Diamond T 968, this truck is in fact a scarce 970A, built for the Canadian military. The truck, which is 16 inches longer than the 968, was photographed in Europe in 1944. (Fred Crismon collection)

A well restored 968 exhibits the closed top found on early-production Diamond T 4-ton trucks. Twenty-two rearward-pointing louvers in the side panels of the hood enhanced ventilation of the engine compartment. (Pat Ware)

The radiator and the headlights on the Diamond T have separate guards. An extension on the left service headlight guard only protected the blackout headlight. Embossed on the center of the radiator tank at the top of the radiator is the Diamond T logo. (Chris Hughes)

Between the members of the chassis frame just behind the front bumper is the front-mounted winch. The gear case is in the foreground, and a canvas cover is secured around the cable drum. The winch was powered by a three-speed takeoff from the transmission. (Chris Hughes)

Details of the front end of a vehicle displayed at the Joe Garbarino Military Museum are viewed from the left. Vehicle specifications called for 10-ply, size 9.00-20 tires with snow and mud treads. The wheels were Budd no. 44460, a tapered-disk design, size 20-8, with holes for 10 mounting lugs. (Chris Hughes)

The assembly between the rear of the hood and the fronts of the cab doors is the cowl. A ventilation door is on each side of the cowl, operable from within the cab by unlatching and pushing it open or pulling it closed. The left ventilation door is shown open. (Chris Hughes)

Below the driver's door on the left side of the cab is a 60-gallon fuel tank with a filler cap on top. The top of the fuel tank also serves as a step and is fitted with a nonslip diamond tread panel. At the bottom of the tank is a running board, also with diamond tread. (Chris Hughes)

A five-gallon liquid container is stowed in a holder mounted on the front of the front left splash shield, sometimes called a mud guard. The splash shield assemblies were fabricated from sheet metal with three vertical stiffeners formed into them. (Chris Hughes)

The left side of the early closed-type, or hardtop, cab is displayed. The door is mounted on three hinges, with the operating handle to the rear of the door. A rear-view mirror is mounted above the top hinge, and a grab handle is on the cab to the rear of the door. (Chris Hughes)

The operating handle of the left door and the grab handle, designed to help the driver hoist himself up to the door, are viewed close-up. Visible at the front of the cargo body is a spare tire. Two spare-tire carriers were included to the front of the cargo body. (Chris Hughes)

The inside of the door of a closed-type cab of a Diamond T 4-ton truck is displayed. In addition to the door latch-operating handle at the center of the door below the side window, a fairly dainty window operating crank handle was included. (Chris Hughes)

The steering wheel of this Diamond T once had an olive-drab finish, part of which is still present, but most of which has worn off down to the black hard rubber below the finish. On the hub of the steering wheel is the horn button with the Diamond T logo on it. (Chris Hughes)

The steering wheel and driver's seat cushion are viewed through the driver's open door. The driver's seat cushion rested in an adjustable frame, enabling the driver to adjust the height of the seat by placing its mounting lugs in the proper holes in the frame. The foot-operated button on the floor toward the lower bottom is the cranking motor switch, for starting the engine. It was positioned so the driver could depress it with his right heel. The device on the side of the steering column is a non-original turn signal switch. (Chris Hughes)

7

The cranking motor switch is seen close-up. Also in view are, left to right, the clutch pedal, the bottom of the steering column, the brake pedal, the accelerator pedal, and, on top of the tunnel, the lower part of the transmission gear shift lever and its boot. (Chris Hughes)

A driver's-eye view shows the arrangement of the clutch pedal (left) and brake pedal (right) to either side of the lower part of the steering column. The small button on the floor to the left of the clutch pedal is the dimmer switch for the service headlights. (Chris Hughes)

The horn button on the steering wheel hub has the Diamond T logo. To the left of the horn button is a non-original turn-signal switch. Partially visible to the right of the horn button is the hand lever for controlling the air brakes on a towed gun or trailer. (Chris Hughes)

The military-type instrument panel is viewed from slightly below. At the top center is the dash light, with the main light switch to the left of it. The tachometer is to the left. Below the instrument panel is the operating lever for the ventilation door on top of the cowl. (Chris Hughes)

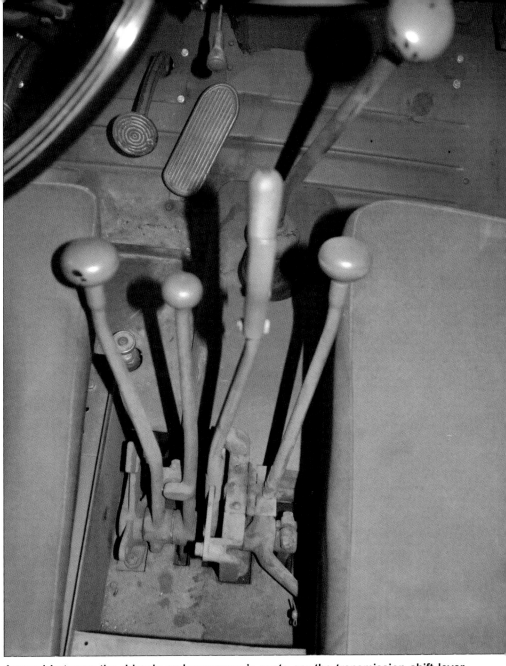

Above the instrument panel are two data plates. The rectangular plate at left lists three relevant publications that were to be issued with the truck: the vehicle's Ordnance Parts List, operator's manual, and maintenance manual. The square plate provides transmission-shift and power takeoff instructions. (Chris Hughes)

The two windshield panels of the closed-type cab were hinged so that they could be swung open for ventilation. Two slotted arms fitted with wing nuts held each panel open. Seen here are the two inboard arms of the windshields and the right windshield wiper. (Chris Hughes)

Arrayed between the driver's and passenger's seats are the transmission shift lever (upper right), and, to its rear, (left to right), the transfer case shift lever, the declutching lever, the handbrake lever, and the power takeoff (PTO) shift lever. The declutching lever was used to engage or disengage the front axle drive. The transfer case shift lever was set on low when the vehicle was starting on a grade or was heavily loaded, and on high when starting on level ground or lightly loaded. (Chris Hughes)

As seen through the passenger's door, the hand lever for controlling the air brakes on a towed gun or trailer is prominent on the right side of the steering column. On the right side of the dash is a windshield wiper control; another one is on the left side of the dash. (Chris Hughes)

The front seats, steering wheel, control levers, and instrument panel are observed from the passenger's door. Separate seats remained a feature throughout all models of the Diamond T 4-ton trucks, to allow room for the control levers between the seats. (Chris Hughes)

The ceiling of the cab of a closed-top Diamond T is seen from the passenger's door. The oblong opening to the right is the glove box, which was not supplied with a door. Immediately to the rear of the glove box are two roof-ventilator doors with knobs. (Chris Hughes)

At the center of the rear wall of the closed-top Diamond T is a small window. The screws with square nuts arranged around the window are for holding in place the wire-screen guard visible through the window. A vertical stiffener is to each side of the window. (Chris Hughes)

The brass-colored equipment is a one-quart fire extinguisher, stored in a holder on the inside of the cowl to the front of the passenger's seat. Also in view are some details of the floor boards and the area below the dash on the passenger's side of the cab. (Chris Hughes)

The early-type metal cargo body is viewed from adjacent to the driver's door, facing to the rear. Inverted hooks are attached at intervals around the cargo body for tying down the tarpaulin cover. A reflector is on the front corner of the cargo body. (Chris Hughes)

The spare tires at the front of the cargo body are observed. Each of the wheels is fastened to its carrier with three nuts and screws. Also in view are the front ends of the troop seats, fabricated from wooden slats, and the stakes, with wooden slats fastened to them. (Chris Hughes)

The grab handle and the driver's door-operating handle are viewed close-up. The grab handle is attached to the cab with four flat-headed, slotted screws, two at the top and two below. To the right are the left spare tire and its carrier at the front of the cargo body. (Chris Hughes)

The protective screen over the rear window of the cab is seen in detail. Atop the cab is the roof ventilator shell, a feature of the closed-cab Diamond T 4-ton trucks. A filter in the roof ventilator kept dust from circulating into the cab. (Chris Hughes)

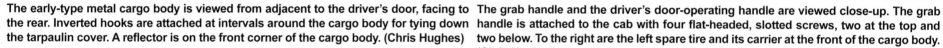

The cab roof ventilator shell, as viewed from the left rear, was removable, seated on a sponge-rubber gasket. Two inlet louvers are on the top of the shell. Also in view is part of the top of the hood and the left fender, with a diamond-tread panel to the rear of the headlight. (Chris Hughes)

The cab roof ventilator shell and the cab body are observed from the right rear. The roof of the cab body was a one-piece assembly fabricated from pressed steel. To the right, a diamond-tread panel is present atop the right fender, the same as on the left fender. (Chris Hughes)

The early-production cargo body had a steel floor in addition to steel side panels. Later Diamond T 4-ton cargo bodies would feature wooden floors and side panels. Two spare tires are shown in their stowed positions at the front end of the cargo body. (Chris Hughes)

The rear of an early-production all-steel cargo body is displayed. The body is equipped with a steel tailgate with hinges at the bottom. The two U-shaped fittings fastened to the top of the tailgate are steps to assist troops in climbing up onto the cargo bed. (Chris Hughes)

The right side of the early-production steel cargo body is shown. Stake pockets are built into the side of the body, to accept the removable stakes. The tandem rear suspensions featured 10-ply, size 9.00-20 tires with snow and mud treads, mounted in pairs. (Chris Hughes)

The front left splash shield, or mud guard, of the steel cargo body is viewed facing forward. Two braces are attached to the shield and to the cross member of the chassis frame. The four nuts and screws at the bottom secure the liquid container holder. (Chris Hughes)

Looking across the chassis from behind the front left splash shield, the propeller shaft from the transfer case (left) back to the forward rear axle is prominent. The transfer case was mounted directly behind the transmission and had two speeds: direct and overdrive. (Chris Hughes)

The two left sets of rear tires are viewed. The outer wheels of the dual-wheel sets were mounted with the dished, or concave, side facing outward. Between the tires are the left torque rod bracket and the center part of the leaf spring, including the U-bolts. (Chris Hughes)

14

Toward the rear of the left side of the chassis frame is a service air line attached to a dummy coupling, which protected the line's coupling when not in use. There were service air lines on each side of the frame, providing compressed air to towed units. (Chris Hughes)

The steel cargo body of a closed-top Diamond T 4-ton truck is observed from the left rear. In addition to the U-shaped steps fastened to the top of the tailgate, steps were also attached to the aft sides of the rear splash shields; the center step is missing on this one. (Chris Hughes)

Below the tailgate is the cross-sill or body bolster; at its center is the door for a toolbox, fitted with a padlock. Also on the cross-sill are holes to accommodate tail light assemblies (not present) and the a flip-up cover for the towed-unit electrical connection. (Chris Hughes)

At the rear of the chassis between the bumperettes is the pintle hook. The hook is turned upside down, with the assembly's lock, normally oriented at the top of the hook, dangling below it. This hook would have been used to tow artillery pieces or trailers. (Chris Hughes)

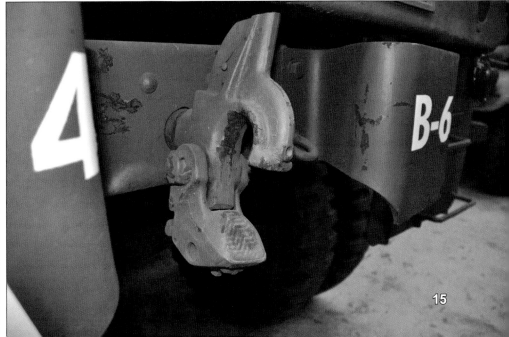

15

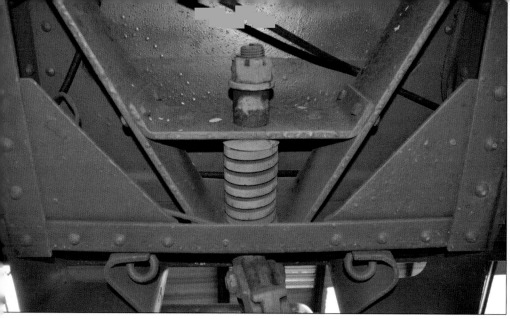

The pintle hook is visible at the bottom of this view upward at the rear of the chassis frame. The shaft of the pintle hook is fitted with a coil spring that provides buffering action to the assembly. The front of the shaft is secured with a nut to a support attached to a V-shaped brace. (Chris Hughes)

The differential carrier of the Timken rear tandem axle, mounted atop the axle housing, is viewed facing aft. The differential carriers were of through-shaft design, with a propeller shaft transferring power from the carrier of the forward tandem axle to the rear one. (Chris Hughes)

The right half of the rear Timken tandem axle is observed, facing forward. Both tandem axles were fitted with Bendix Westinghouse service brakes, leaf springs, and torque rods, seen here attached to the torsion rod bracket on the axle, to maintain axle alignment. (Chris Hughes)

A view of the left side of the rear tandem axle emphasizes details of the torsion rod bracket and the leaf spring's contact with the spring plate on top of the axle housing. Grease fittings for brake mechanisms are adjacent to the torsion rod bracket. (Chris Hughes)

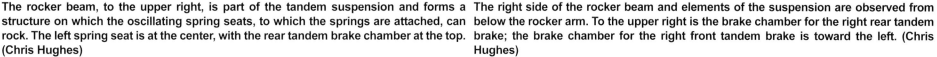

The rocker beam, to the upper right, is part of the tandem suspension and forms a structure on which the oscillating spring seats, to which the springs are attached, can rock. The left spring seat is at the center, with the rear tandem brake chamber at the top. (Chris Hughes)

The right side of the rocker beam and elements of the suspension are observed from below the rocker arm. To the upper right is the brake chamber for the right rear tandem brake; the brake chamber for the right front tandem brake is toward the left. (Chris Hughes)

The tailgate has four hinges at the bottom. A long hinge pin passes through all four hinges and is secured at each end with a cotter pin. Two hooks for securing a tarpaulin over the cargo body are fastened to the rear of the tailgate. Reflectors are also present. (Chris Hughes)

Near the rear of the right side of the chassis frame is a service air line attached to a dummy coupling, similar to the arrangement on the left side of the frame shown earlier. These lines provided compressed air to operate the brakes of towed artillery or trailers. (Chris Hughes)

The service air line couplings mounted on the side of the chassis frame were sometimes nicknamed "glad hands." The shield braces and the fasteners and square reinforcement tabs that hold the three steps in place on the rear of the splash shield are in view. (Chris Hughes)

Between the right rear tandem tires is the assembly containing the right torque rod bracket and spring seat. Cast into the torque rod bracket, upside down, are "Timken" as well as casting numbers and other marks. Timken also manufactured the torque rods. (Chris Hughes)

The front right splash shield and its two braces are viewed here from behind. To the lower left of the splash shield are the exhaust tailpipe and the rear of the muffler. The tailpipe bracket was a simple metal strip with a right-angle twist near the bottom. (Chris Hughes)

As on the front left splash shield, a holder for a 5-gallon liquid container was mounted on the front of the front right splash shield. On the near side of the liquid container is a metal strip that acts as a reinforcement tab for the connection point of the splash shield brace. (Chris Hughes)

The front right corner of the steel cargo body is viewed, showing the various components and weld seams that make up its construction. On the front panel of the cargo body are a reflector and a hook for securing a tarpaulin; two more hooks are visible on the right side of the steel cargo body. (Chris Hughes)

The battery box is below the passenger's door. The battery box is fitted with a door with a piano hinge at its front edge and, at its rear, a clasp with a wing nut to secure the battery-box door closed. Inside the box were two 6-volt batteries wired in a series parallel circuit. (Chris Hughes)

The battery box door is viewed from another angle. A diamond-tread nonslip pattern is present on the running board as well as on the step formed by the top of the battery box. The left cowl ventilation door is visible to the front of the passenger's door. (Chris Hughes)

The positions and layout of the grab handle, mounted on the right rear corner of the cab, and of the door-operating handle mirror the positions and layout of similar handles on the left side of the cab. Also in view here is the right spare tire and the front side of its storage rack at the front of the cargo body. (Chris Hughes)

The passenger's door has an adjustable rear-view mirror on a telescoping arm mounted above the top door hinge. The Diamond T 4-ton ordnance supply catalogs referred to the exterior door handles for closed-top cabs as "handle, cab door, outside." (Chris Hughes)

The passenger's door of a closed-top cab is open, revealing details of the interior of the door. Ordnance supply catalogs for the Diamond T 4-ton trucks referred to the interior door handles on closed-cab models as "handle, cab door, remote control." (Chris Hughes)

The interior of the closed-top cab is viewed through the passenger's door, showing details of the passenger's seat cushion or pad and seat back, also referred to in the ordnance supply catalogs as a lazyback. Also in view are the steering wheel and various controls. (Chris Hughes)

A close-up view shows the window operating crank and interior door handle on a closed-top cab's passenger door. Ordnance supply catalog terminology for the door window operating crank seen at the left was "handle, cab door window regulator." (Chris Hughes)

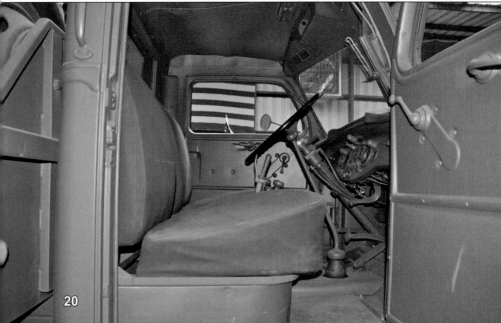

The rear-view mirror on the passenger's side door of the closed-top cab is viewed from the front. At the middle of the telescoping arm of the mirror is the thumbscrew for locking the arm at the desired length. Two brackets hold the base of the arm. (Chris Hughes)

The base of the rear-view mirror arm is affixed with a horizontal screw and hex cap nut to a T-shaped fitting that rests in the two brackets fastened to the door. This arrangement allowed the mirror arm to be adjusted upward and downward and from front to rear. (Chris Hughes)

The front end of the closed-cab Diamond T 4-ton cargo truck is observed from the right side. Below the fender assembly is a steel panel with louvers in it, called the fender shield. Alongside the fender shield are two of the three irons, fender-support brackets. (Chris Hughes)

A piano hinge is on the interior of the hood along the joint between the louvered side panel of the hood and the top panel of the hood. Grab handles are at the front and rear of the side panel. (Chris Hughes)

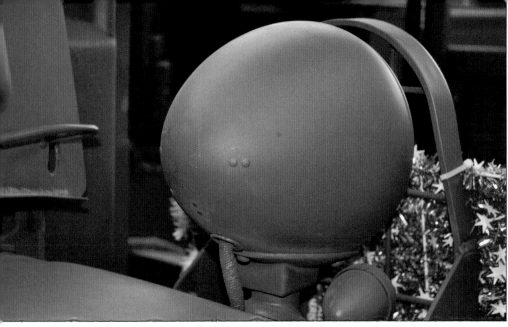

The rear of the housing of the right service headlight is displayed, along with the braided electrical cable that supplied power to it. To the right of the service headlight is the right blackout marker lamp, for indicating the position of the truck during blackout conditions. (Chris Hughes)

The right service headlight and blackout marker lamp are observed from the right side, with the brush guard to the front of them. The brush guards were designed with triangular pieces on the sides that served both as braces and mounting brackets for the guards. (Chris Hughes)

The Timken double-reduction-drive "banjo" axle is viewed from the front. Projecting from the front of the case is the lubricant filler plug. To the right, next to the left wheel, is the steering arm. The front springs, spring brackets, and engine oil pan also are in view. (Chris Hughes)

Looking up from under the front of the chassis, the underside of the winch is in view. The cable drum has a canvas cover. The winch propeller shaft is to the left, above the spring bracket, and is connected at the rear to the transfer case. To the right is another vehicle. (Chris Hughes)

The top of the same winch seen in the preceding photo is viewed from the right side, with the front bumper to the right and the radiator guard to the left. The winch cable was approximately 300 feet long, and had a safe-pull capacity of 15,000 pounds. (Chris Hughes)

The steel-slat construction of the radiator guard is illustrated. To the rear of the slats is a horizontal reinforcing bar to maintain the slats' alignment. On the front of the radiator tank at the top is the Diamond T logo. In the background is the left headlight guard. (Chris Hughes)

The left headlight guard and headlights cluster are observed from the front. A C-shaped extension of the headlight guard provided some protection to the blackout headlight, next to the radiator. Below the service headlight is the left blackout marker lamp. (Chris Hughes)

The upper part of the radiator assembly is displayed. The radiator had a finned-tube-type core and a frontal area of 636 square inches and thickness of 3 inches. On the top tank is the filler cap, with a single lever to assist in turning it. Not visible here is the bottom tank. (Chris Hughes)

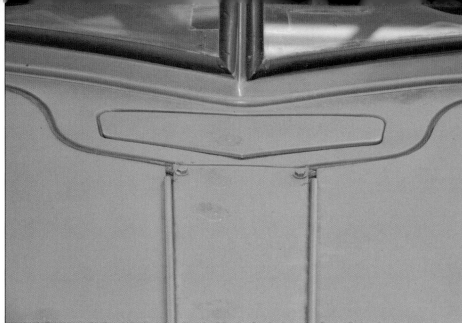

At the center of the top of the hood is a stationary member to which the two upper sections of hood are joined with hinges. Similarly, the side panels of the hood, not seen here, are hinged to the top panels and rise up with the top panels when the hood is raised. (Chris Hughes)

At the top center of the cowl is a ventilator door that, when opened, would provide fresh air to the cab. This ventilator door was present on both closed-top and open-top Diamond T 4-ton trucks and was operated remotely from inside the cab by means of a control. (Chris Hughes)

The windshield panels of the closed-top Diamond T 4-ton trucks were set into rubber gaskets around the windshield openings. Each windshield had a wiper; the left wiper is missing on this vehicle. Above the windshield is the roof ventilator assembly. (Chris Hughes)

The front of the roof ventilator found on closed-cab Diamond T 4-ton trucks forms the air intake. The bottom rim of the ventilator shell is set into a sponge-rubber gasket. Two louvers are on top of the shell. This ventilator was an automatic intake and exhaust type. (Chris Hughes)

Open-top cabs started coming into production for Diamond T 4-ton cargo trucks in the summer of 1943. This example is displayed with the windshield raised, but the canvas tarpaulin is not installed over the cab. A full set of stakes is installed on the cargo body.

The right service headlight and its brush guard are seen from an angle. "Prestone 45" stenciled on the top tank of the radiator replicates a practice in the U.S. Army of marking on its vehicles the year when antifreeze was added to the radiator fluid: in this case, 1945.

The blackout marker lamp is visible from this angle outboard of the right service headlight. The crosspieces of the brush guard are made of heavy steel wire, with the vertical pieces set in front of, and with bends to fit around, the horizontal pieces.

The Diamond T 4-ton cargo truck with open-top cab features a windshield assembly that can be folded down and stored on the hood. Displayed on the right fender is a bridge-classification symbol. The "ASCZ 359" on the right side of the bumper stands for Advance Section, Communications Zone 359. The chain wrapped around the bumper is attached to the winch cable.

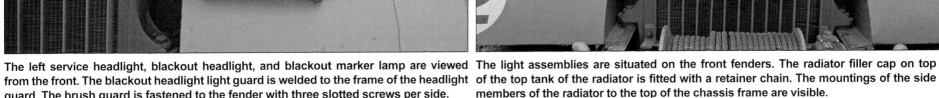

The left service headlight, blackout headlight, and blackout marker lamp are viewed from the front. The blackout headlight light guard is welded to the frame of the headlight guard. The brush guard is fastened to the fender with three slotted screws per side.

The light assemblies are situated on the front fenders. The radiator filler cap on top of the top tank of the radiator is fitted with a retainer chain. The mountings of the side members of the radiator to the top of the chassis frame are visible.

Behind the bumper is the front-mounted Gar Wood winch. At the center is the cable drum; toward the left side of the chassis frame is the top of the gear box. Below the bumper is the casing for the winch brake. A data plate is atop the gear box.

Looking under the front bumper, in the foreground are the winch cable drum and winch brake housing. Cast directly onto each side of the Timken axle housing are fittings through which the U-bolts that secure the axle to the springs fit.

A Diamond T 4-ton truck with open-top cab and cargo body is viewed from the left side. Unlike, for example, the GMC CCKW 2½ ton truck with open-top cab, which did not have hard doors on the cab, the Diamond Ts had metal doors mounted on piano hinges.

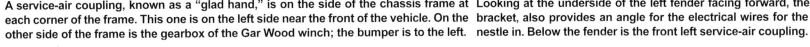

A service-air coupling, known as a "glad hand," is on the side of the chassis frame at each corner of the frame. This one is on the left side near the front of the vehicle. On the other side of the frame is the gearbox of the Gar Wood winch; the bumper is to the left.

Looking at the underside of the left fender facing forward, the front iron, or mounting bracket, also provides an angle for the electrical wires for the left headlight cluster to nestle in. Below the fender is the front left service-air coupling.

The left fender shield, a sheet-metal panel with ventilation louvers in it, is viewed close-up. The underside of the top of the left fender is at the top of the photograph. Two stiffeners are attached to the underside of the fender to reinforce the thin sheet metal.

Just forward of the bottom of the rear iron of the left fender is the fuel filter, which has a filter element inside the bowl at the bottom. To the rear of the fuel filter is the Pitman arm, which acts on the drag link to push and pull the steering arm to steer the wheels.

The Diamond T 4-ton truck with open-top cab and cargo body is observed from the left side. Open-top cabs saved on shipping bulk and made it easy to install an M36 antiaircraft machine gun ring mount over the cab.

The side panels of the hood have 22 rear-pointing ventilation louvers. Marked on the edge of the fender is the specified tire pressure, 65 p.s.i. Such tire pressure stencilling was not used during World War II.

A 5-gallon liquid container is in its holder on the front left splash shield. The channel that is tack-welded to the rear corner of the cab is a bracket for attaching a stanchion to support a machine gun ring mount. U-bolts would fasten the stanchion to the bracket.

A pioneer tool rack was provided on the side of the fuel tank for storing a single-bit axe; a No. 2 general-purpose, D-handled shovel; and a Type 2, Class F mattock head and handle. The implements are secured by brackets and webbing straps with buckles.

Details of the pioneer tool rack, the liquid container and its holder, the lower part of the ring-mount bracket, and the front left corner of the steel cargo body are displayed. Tack welding was used to fasten the side panel of the cargo body to the side sill of the body.

Underneath the chassis frame, as viewed from the front of the left forward tandem tires, part of the transfer case is in view, along with the propeller shaft leading back to the front tandem axle. The coil spring toward the bottom is the release spring of the parking brake.

In a continuation of the preceding photograph but looking aft, the propeller shaft connects to the differential carrier of the forward tandem axle. In the background is the inter-axle propeller shaft, leading from the carrier in the foreground to the carrier of the aft axle.

From this angle, the rear end of the open-type-cab version of the Diamond T 4-ton truck with the steel cargo body appears quite similar in appearance to that of the closed-type-cab example shown earlier in this book. Unit markings are on the bumperettes.

The rear of the aft tandem axle is displayed. Secured with hex nuts to the top of the axle housing is the differential carrier. Attached to the bottom of the chassis frame above the springs are spring-stop plates. Details of the torque rods also are visible.

In a view of the rear of a Diamond T 4-ton truck with the open-type cab, the two spare tires stored on their carriers at the front of the cargo body are visible above the tailgate. Steps are attached to the top of the tailgate. The rear splash shields are not present.

The two spare tires are shown on their storage mounts on the front panel of the cargo body. The troop seats along the sides have been raised, and the seat supports are dangling from the seats. The floor of the cargo bed was fabricated of welded steel.

To each side of the tool box door below the tailgate are tail light assemblies, and to the left of the door is the receptacle for an electrical connection for a towed unit. On the left bumperette is a unit marking for Advance Section, Communications Zone 359S.

The right troop seats are shown in the raised position. The seat supports were attached to the troop seats with swivel-type mounts; when the seats were lowered, the supports inclined at an angle, with the bottoms resting against the side panel of the body.

Since the troop seats are shorter than the two horizontal slats attached to the tops of the stakes, in order to provide clearance for the spare tires, when the seats are in the raised position, there is a gap between the front of the seats and the forward stake.

The rear side of the front right splash shield is displayed, showing its two braces and the three V-shaped channels built into the shield, which act to reinforce the sheet-metal construction. To the rear of the splash shield are the tail pipe and its bracket.

On the all-steel cargo body, these lateral braces were welded to the chassis frame (left), the floor plates (top), and the side sill of the body (right), to provide structural support for the floor and the side of the body. These braces are on the right side of the vehicle.

The door of the battery box on this open-cab Diamond T has replica U.S. Port Agency War Shipping Administration markings, giving vehicular weight and dimensions. On the rear corner of the cab is a mounting bracket for a machine gun ring mount.

Two mounting brackets for a machine gun ring mount are visible in this photograph; to the far left and immediately to the front of the passenger's door, below the rear-view mirror. As on closed-top cabs, grab handles were provided on the open-top cabs.

The thin metal panel with diamond-tread surface attached to the front right fender is seen from adjacent to the passenger's door. When a G.I. had to climb on top of the fender to work on the engine during wet weather, this panel helped him keep from slipping off.

The rear of the right fender and the rear iron, or fender mounting bracket, are displayed. The iron is fastened to the right spring hanger, which acts as a mounting bracket for the suspension spring. The rear spring shackle is to the lower front of the spring hanger.

Looking upward from the view in the preceding photograph, the right spring hanger is to the left, and above it is the center fender iron. Below the bottom of the iron, on the underside of the frame is a plate that limited the upward travel of the spring.

The center fender iron and the front fender iron are visible on the right side of the vehicle. Immediately below the front iron is the right shock absorber. The round part of the shock was called the instrument; a rod extends from the arm of the instrument to the axle.

The rear part of the right front spring is shown in detail. To the right are the U-bolts that secure the spring to the axle; on top of the spring between the U-bolts is a spacer with a bumper on top. At the top center is the spring plate, and to the left is the spring hanger.

Details of the right front wheel and tire are shown. As with closed-type-cab Diamond T 4-ton trucks, open-cab versions specified 10-ply, size 9.00-20 tires with snow and mud treads, mounted on Budd no. 44460 wheels, a tapered-disk design, size 20-8.

The right shock absorber is shown close-up, including the operating arm and the rod from the arm to the axle. At the center is the outboard side of the spring bracket, to the front of which is the right front service-air coupling line and bracket.

The right service headlight, blackout marker lamp, and headlight brush guard are viewed from the right. To the left is the nonslip plate atop the fender. To the right is the front-mounted winch. A tow hook is bolted to the chassis frame on each side of the winch.

Sheet metal panels attached to the top of the front bumper and frame rails provide a surface upon which personnel can stand while performing engine maintenance. The panels also prevent mud and debris from being thrown onto the front of the truck.

The top radiator tank, the filler cap, and the overflow tube are viewed close-up. Behind the radiator cap are the two hex screws that secure the front of the stationary member of the hood in place; two screws for the same purpose are at the rear of the member.

Directly to the front of the cowl ventilator door at the bottom of the photo are the two hex screws at the rear of the stationary member of the hood. Also on that member is a hold-down latch and rubber bumper for the windshield when it is in the lowered position.

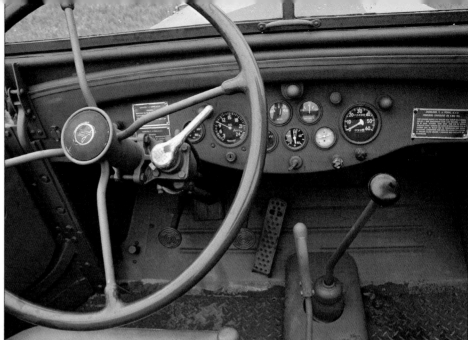

Two M1 Garand .30-caliber rifles are in the rifle rack to the far left in the open-type cab. The interior of the driver's door is visible as well. On the side of the steering column is the control for operating the brakes of towed units.

This vehicle's data plates are in Danish, as many surplus tactical vehicles went to U.S. allies under the 1949 Mutual Defense Assistance Act. Also visible are the instrument panel (with gauges in English), the transmission shift lever, and the handbrake lever.

The Hercules RXC engine of a Diamond T cargo truck is seen from the right in a 3 March 1944 photograph. The carburetor is in the center foreground, at the center of the cylinder heads. On the firewall to the left is the waterproof generator voltage regulator.

The Hercules RXC engine is viewed from the left side in a 3 March 1944 photograph. At the center is the engine air cleaner, to the rear of which are the two engine oil filters. Between the air cleaner and the radiator is the crankcase breather filter.

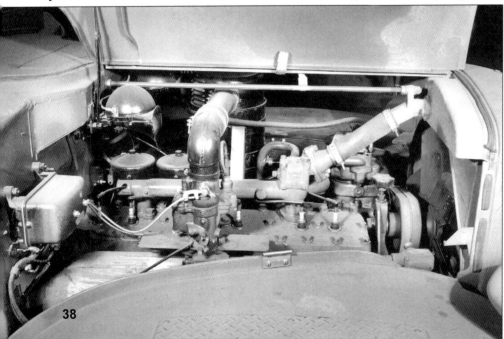

The 4-ton truck's long-wheelbase ponton transport versions were designated models 970 and 970A. It can be distinguished by the space between the rear of the cab and the front of the cargo body.

While the tailgate of this long-wheelbase Diamond T 970A with a wooden cargo body appears to be authentic, the bolster below the tailgate seems to be a makeshift replacement part, lacking a recessed toolbox and having the tail light assemblies mounted below it.

This Diamond T 970A has the wooden cargo body that superseded the early all-steel cargo bodies. A good view is available of the bracket at the rear corner of the cab for installing an M36 machine gun ring mount. This example is a model 970A, with military instruments. The 970s were produced for the Canadians.

The floor of a wooden cargo body is viewed looking forward from the right rear corner. Steel strips are fastened between each plank of the floor. Spare-tire carriers are not present at the front of the cargo body, having been moved forward of the cargo body.

Diamond T produced a line of wreckers based on the 4-ton chassis and designated models 969, 969A, and 969B. The basic 969, a closed-cab design, was modified with military-type instruments and filters to become the 969A, and the 969B was an export version with a single headlight and single taillight. Shown here is a Model 969A with a closed-type cab and a Holmes W-45 H.D. military wrecker bed with twin booms and two 5-ton winches restored by Steve Greenberg. The wrecker bed had side panels with a distinctive tapered or beveled front end. Markings on the fenders are for the 479th Amphibious Truck Company, 1st Engineer Special Brigade. (James Alexander)

This vehicle exhibits a field modification sometimes seen on Diamond T wreckers: to extend the front bumper downward, another bumper has been turned upside down and fastened beneath the stock bumper. This arangement allowed the wrecker to push a CCKW without overriding the GMC's bumper or bumperettes. (James Alexander)

Like the cargo-body Diamond T 4-ton trucks, the wrecker versions mounted a Gar Wood Model 3U-615 winch at the front of the chassis frame. To the right is the gearbox of the winch, containing the worm drive. On top of the gearbox is a Gar Wood data plate. (James Alexander)

The bottom of the cable drum of the front winch is seen through the gap between the two front bumpers. The drum carried 300 feet of ⅝-inch steel cable. Powered by a shaft from the power takeoff, the winch had a rated capacity of 15,000 pounds. (James Alexander)

Fastened with hex screws and nuts to the bottom of the right chassis frame next to the winch drum is a steel bracket for mounting the extra lower front bumper. The rear of the bracket was carefully cut to fit around the front right spring bracket, seen to the right.

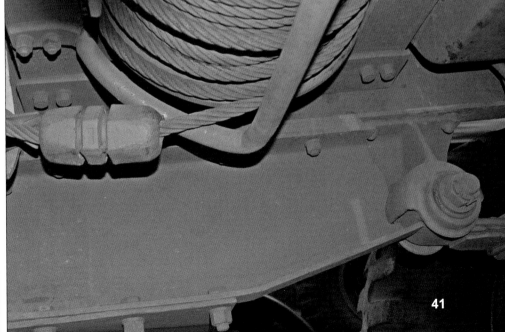

The left mounting bracket of the extra front bumper is viewed. In the background is the left front wheel and tire. At the top right is the worm-gear case of the winch, to the rear of which is the propeller shaft from the winch back to the power takeoff assembly.

Under the left fender is the red "glad hand" service air coupling. The three irons that support the fender are all in view. To the right is the spring shackle and hanger. Above the tire are the shock absorber and the fuel filter. (James Alexander)

The left front service-air line and coupling and the shock absorber are viewed close-up. Also displayed are the outside of the bracket for the extra bumper and, to the lower left of the photo, a steel gusset plate attached to the bumper and the bumper bracket. (James Alexander)

Under the left fender are the fender shield (top) and, left to right, the brake hose, fuel filter, limit plate for the spring, center fender iron, Pitman arm, and spring hanger and shackle. The tube attached to the bottom of the Pitman arm is the drag link. (James Alexander)

Each fender was fabricated from an inboard and outboard section, with a joint running lengthwise. Atop that joint is a Mars safety light, often seen in that position on military wrecker trucks. Details of the headlights and headlight brush guard also are in view. (James Alexander)

The Mars flashing safety light is viewed close-up from above. The plate affixed to the housing reads, "Manufactured by / Mars Signal Light Company / Chicago Illinois." The pattern of the diamond-tread non-slip panel on the fender is also visible in this image. (James Alexander)

General Data

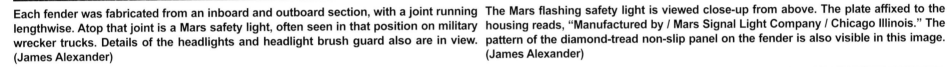

MODEL	WRECKER	CARGO	DUMP	PONTON
WEIGHT, EMPTY	21,700 pounds	18,400 pounds	17,725 pounds	18,800 pounds
WEIGHT, LOADED	–	26,400 pounds	25,725 pounds	26,800 pounds
MAX TOWED LOAD	25,000 pounds	25,000 pounds	25,000 pounds	25,000 pounds
LENGTH	291.625 inches	297 inches	264.625 inches	297 inches
WIDTH	99.5 inches	95.25 inches	94 inches	96 inches
HEIGHT	116 inches	119 inches	106 inches	119 inches
TRACK	72 inches	72 inches	72 inches	72 inches
TIRE SIZE	9.00-20	9.00-20	9.00-20	9.00-20
MAX SPEED	40 mph	40 mph	40 mph	40 mph
FUEL CAPACITY	60 gallons	60 gallons	60 gallons	60 gallons
RANGE	180 miles	180 miles	180 miles	180 miles
ELECTRICAL	6/12 positive	6/12 positive	6/12 positive	6/12 positive
TRANSMISSION SPEEDS	5	5	5	5
TRANSFER SPEEDS	2	2	2	2
TURNING RADIUS	32.5 R / 34 L feet	37.5 R / 39 L feet	32.5 R / 34 L feet	37.5 R / 39 L feet

A Diamond T wrecker with a closed-type cab is seen from the left side. The exterior of the cab was similar to those of Diamond T 4-ton closed-cab cargo trucks. The wrecker assembly featured a crane supporting two movable booms and two winches called service drums. The twin booms could be swung out to a right angle to the side of the vehicle, giving them the ability to lift objects to the sides of the vehicle as well as to the rear. To stabilize the wrecker when the booms were operated to the sides, brace legs were mounted on each side of the top of the crane, which were lowered and firmly planted on the ground on the side on which the boom was to be working. (James Alexander)

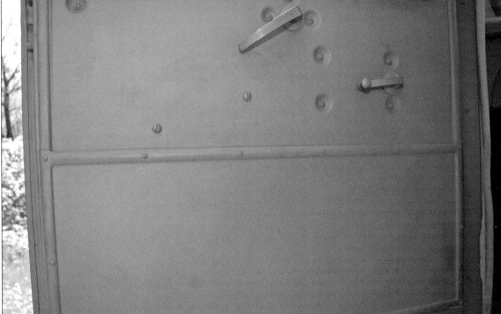

The interior of the driver's door is displayed. At the upper center is the interior door-operating handle, officially called the "handle, cab door, remote control." Below and forward of that handle is the crank handle for raising and lowering the window. (James Alexander)

The forward part of the left side of the wrecker body is shown. At the center, immediately to the rear of the left brace leg, is the base, or heel, of the left boom. Next to the boom, to the front of the spare tire, is the independent air compressor, driven by a gasoline engine. (James Alexander)

This wrecker cab has been fitted with reupholstered seats with a reddish material. As this vehicle lacked the cab-roof ventilator, ventilator doors are not present to the rear of the open glove box in the ceiling. A musette with the U.S. Army Engineers insignia on it rests on the passenger's seat. The usual control levers were between the seats, and on the floor directly in front of the base of the seat is the siren footswitch. (James Alexander)

In a view of the left side of the crane, the entire length of the left brace leg is shown. A chain wrapped around the lower part of the leg secures it in place. Next to the top of the brace leg is a snatch block. Oxygen and acetylene bottles for welding use are secured in place to the rear of the cab. The bottle with the green cap contains oxygen, while the one with the red cap holds acetylene. (James Alexander)

The circular object between the brace leg and the acetylene bottle is the left service drum, which held the winch cable. There is a service drum for each boom. A roller chain from the power takeoff drove the wrecker transmission, which in turn drove the service drums. The booms were raised and lowered by a hand crank inserted in the ratcheting mechanism on the heel of the boom. (James Alexander)

From this angle, the gears on the inboard side of the left service drum are visible. At the bottom of the drum is a pinion which turned against the gears to operate the service drum. The pinion received its power from a shaft from the wrecker transmission. The wrecker boom had a capacity of 5 tons, or 10 tons when a snatch block was employed. The spare tire is stored on two diagonal braces called stiff legs. (James Alexander)

Between the uprights of the crane is an independent air compressor for inflating tires. Several different compressors were used: the Curtiss, the Kellogg, and the de Vilbiss. Each had a single-cylinder, four-stroke gasoline engine by Briggs & Stratton or Johnson, which drove the compressor by a V-belt. The unit was fastened to the wrecker body with screws through the four feet that supported the air tank. (James Alexander)

A compressor is viewed from its left front quarter. The black data plate on the base plate of the compressor identifies it as by de Vilbiss. On the other side of the compressor is the flywheel guard. At the top of the photo is the spare tire on its carrier on the stiff legs.

A de Vilbiss independent compressor is viewed from the left side of the vehicle facing toward the front of the wrecker, showing the flywheel, the flywheel guard, the compressed air tank, and the feet welded to the bottom of the air tank.

A de Vilbiss independent compressor unit is viewed from above, with the left side of the vehicle in the background. Closest to the bottom of the photo are the compressor and its air cleaner. The fins on the top of the air compressor and the air line are visible to the right of center. Toward the top of the photograph is the gasoline tank, with a red filler cap. To the left is the wrecker transmission. (James Alexander)

The twin booms of the wrecker are of a distinctive shape, fabricated from a central tube reinforced by a truss assembly. This truss comprises four angle irons that are welded to three spacer plates fitted over the central tube. Although the booms present a rather lightweight appearance, the truss design made them very strong and durable. The design of the side of the wrecker body, with its beveled forward end, is also apparent. (James Alexander)

Stored on a D-ring at the top of the left side of the crane is a snatch block, which, with its hook, could be attached to various points or stationary objects and used in simple-tackle or compound-tackle configurations with the winch or boom cables. Depending on the number of snatch blocks and tackles used, the winches could pull or hoist a significantly greater amount of weight than the rated capacity of the winch. (James Alexander)

The entire Diamond T wrecker truck with a closed-type cab is viewed from the left side. The left boom has been swung out partially; it could be swung to a 90-degree angle to the side of the body. At the end of each boom is a twin boom sheave and, dangling down from the boom, a boom-end cable guide. A cable hook is hanging from the cable next to the side of the wrecker body. Visible below the spare tire is the side of the independent compressor. (James Alexander)

The left side of the wrecker body is viewed from above, with the cab partially visible in the background. To the lower right is the left boom, and the spare tire is to the right. A rope is coiled up on the floor of the wrecker body just forward of the left body box, part of which is visible at the bottom. Toward the top is a spotlight for illuminating the work area at night. (James Alexander)

On each side of the wrecker body is a body box with a cover equipped with a piano hinge, visible toward the right. This box is the left one. A pioneer tool rack was mounted on the cover of each of the body boxes. Present on this one are a shovel, a mattock head and mattock handle, and an axe. The pioneer tools are held in place by brackets and webbing straps. (James Alexander)

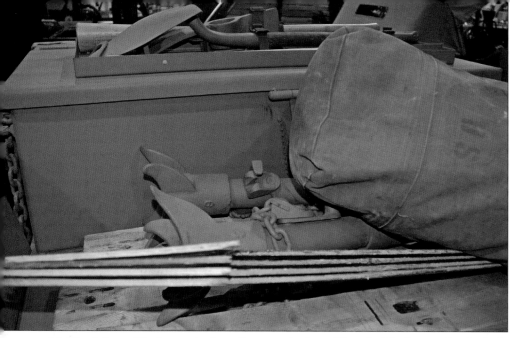

A left bodybox with pioneer tools on its cover is viewed from inside the wrecker body. In the foreground, a duffel bag, a V tow bar, and other items lie on wooden planks on the floor of the wrecker body. To the far left are the tailgate and tailgate chain.

A V tow bar is displayed on the floor of the wrecker body. This is the short-type tow bar used to pull small vehicles, such as Jeeps. The arms were of telescoping construction and could be adjusted for length. The ring would be fastened to the tow hook. (James Alexander)

USA ★ 00807635

479TH AMPH. TRK. CO   1ST ENG. SPEC. BRIG.

The Diamond T wrecker body was fabricated from steel and included a tailgate positioned between the two toolboxes located inside the body. Below the tailgate is the door for the standard recessed toolbox. The angles of the booms when in their stored positions are shown. Unit markings for the 479th Amphibious Truck Company, 1st Engineer Special Brigade, are in white on the bumperettes. The usual three steps are on each of the rear splash shields.

The left bumperette is displayed. In the background, on the side of the bumperette are four mounting screws. Above the bumperette is the cover for the electrical receptacle for a connection to a towed unit. A small spring at the top of the cover kept it closed. (James Alexander)

The right bumperette is seen here. Above it is the right tail light assembly, incorporating a blackout tail light and stop light. To the left is the right side of the toolbox door. Details of the hinges and the single, long hinge pin of the tailgate are also displayed. (James Alexander)

The rear end of the Diamond T wrecker is viewed close-up. The hooks at the ends of the winch cables are secured for transport to safety rings on the cross-sill. In the event that the hoist is inadvertently engaged, placing excess tension on the cables, these rings were designed to release, thus preventing damage to the rear body sill. (James Alexander)

Toward the bottom of the stiff arm is the stiff-arm bolster assembly. The stiff legs are secured to the wrecker body with U-bolts through holes in the bolster. Details of the booms, including the central tubes, spacers, and angle-iron trusses, are in view.

A spare tire is mounted on its carrier on the stiff legs of the crane. On top of the crane are two spotlights for illuminating the work area at night. Outboard of the spotlights are the mast sheaves. To the front of the spare tire, the red cap of an acetylene bottle is visible. (James Alexander)

Resting on the floor of a Diamond T wrecker body is a ground anchor. This was used in certain winching scenarios where it was desirable to run the tackle through a snatch block secured to the anchor. The holes in the channel part were for driving stakes through. (James Alexander)

A section of the right boom is viewed close-up, showing the designs of the spacers that fit over the central tube of the boom. The spacers are welded to the tube and to the angle irons that form the truss of the boom. The bolster of the stiff legs is also in view.

A three-quarters right-rear view of a Diamond T wrecker with the closed-type cab shows the two booms in their stored positions, winch cables secured to the safety rings on the cross-sill, or body bolster. A long tow bar is stored on the side of the body.

To the left is a hand crank employed in raising and lowering the boom. Next to it is an axle clamp. It was fitted to the long tow bar that was stored on the right exterior side of the wrecker bed and was secured to the front axle of a vehicle to be towed. (James Alexander)

The same Diamond T wrecker sits in tall grass. The hooks of the winch cables have been detached from the safety rings on the cross-sill. Pioneer tool racks with complete complements of pioneer tools are present on the covers of both body boxes. On the running board below the passenger's door of the cab is a fire extinguisher, secured in a holder. A large fire extinguisher was part of the standard equipment supplied with wrecker trucks. (James Alexander)

A towbar is in its stored position on the right side of the wrecker body. The eye of the towbar is toward the rear and is held fast in a holder. The other end of the towbar rests in a bracket. When deployed for towing, the eye of the towbar fit over the truck's tow hook. (James Alexander)

The hook of a snatch block is secured to a D-ring at the outer end of the top of the crane. Next to the snatch block are the right twin mast sheaves. They are fitted to a yoke, and protruding to the rear of the yoke is a mast cable guide. Also in view is the right spotlight. (James Alexander)

A close-up view shows the snatch block stowed on the left side of the crane. This snatch block is a single-sheave model. According to the vehicle manual, two snatch blocks were normally to be carried inside the right body box of the wrecker. Some details are also visible of the mast sheaves and the left spotlight. (James Alexander)

The right side of the crane and boom assembly is similar to the left side. A telescoping-type brace leg is attached to the top of the crane and is secured in place with a chain. Next to the brace leg is the right service drum. The ratcheting mechanism of the hand-operated device for lowering and raising the boom is visible toward the heel of the boom. (James Alexander)

The oxygen bottle for the oxy-acetylene welding equipment is secured in place on the other side of the right service drum. Diamond T wreckers had winch controls on each side of the wrecker body. The controls on the right side of the body are below the bottom of the oxygen bottle. Underneath the spare tire is the independent air compressor. (James Alexander)

The original size 9.00-20 tires on this truck were replaced during its restoration with larger 10.00-20 tires. The original 20-inch wheels were used, but the 10.00-20 tires have a one-inch greater section width, and a proportional 1 13/16" increase in diameter as compared to the 9.00-20 tires.

The battery box door is open, providing a view of the two 6-volt batteries. Above the batteries is a compressed air reservoir, part of the brake system. A belt-driven, reciprocating, high-speed compressor provided compressed air for the brake system. (James Alexander)

When in the stored position, the brace leg rests against a U-shaped yoke. Next to the yoke is a D-ring to which the retainer chain for the brace leg is secured. The retainer chain is fitted with a hook, to allow crewmen to quickly detach the chain and deploy the brace leg. Affixed to the bottom of the inner tube of the leg is a circular base plate. (James Alexander)

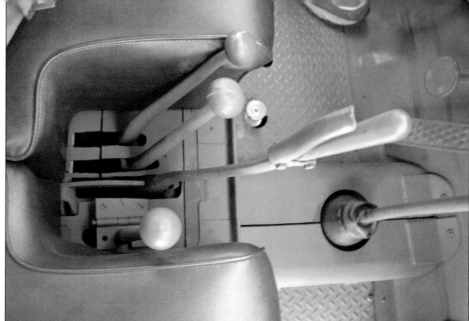

Levers between the seats are for, top to bottom, the transfer-case shift, declutching, handbrake, and PTO shift. The hinge-shaped lock engaged to the PTO lever kept the power takeoff from accidentally being shifted into gear when the winch was not in use. (James Alexander)

The instrument panel of a Diamond T wrecker with closed-type cab is displayed. The large gauge that is the second from the left is the tachometer. The large gauge second from right is the speedometer, below which is the hand throttle control. (James Alexander)

A view inside the passenger's door of a Diamond T wrecker with closed-type cab reveals a musette bag and a hat resting on the passenger's seat. Originally the seat cushions would have been covered with canvas. The two windshield panels are partially opened for ventilation. (James Alexander)

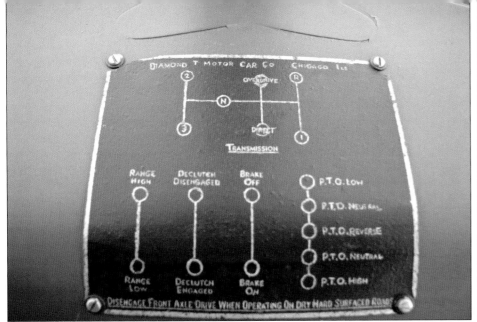

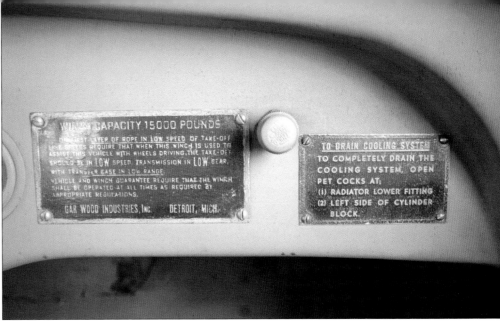

Affixed to the dashboard is this plate with instructions on transmission gearshift patterns on the top, and positions for the transfer case shift lever, the declutching lever, the handbrake lever, and the power takeoff lever to the bottom of the placard. (James Alexander)

On the right side of the dashboard are two instructional plates and a windshield wiper control. The plate on the left concerns the operation of the front-mounted Gar Wood winch, and the one to the right describes how to drain the cooling system. (James Alexander)

Affixed to the dashboard to the front of the steering wheel are instructional plates concerning an alarm signaling the failure of the brakes' air system and the consequences of the sustained operation of the engine at speeds greater than 2,300 rpm. (James Alexander)

This large plate on the driver's side of the cowl provides information on the nomenclature of the vehicle, in this case the Diamond T Model 969A, the serial number (969A5970), and other data. The lower plate lists technical publications for the vehicle. (James Alexander)

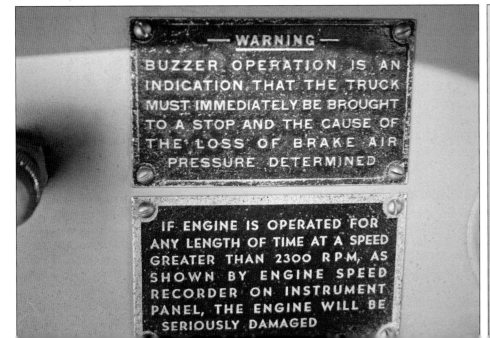

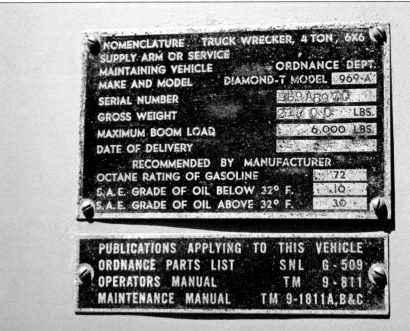

The passenger's door on a closed-cab Diamond T wrecker exhibits some details that differ from those on the cab doors of closed-cab Diamond T 4-ton cargo and troop trucks shown earlier in this book. The escutcheon between the window-operating handle and the door was no longer present, and there was a different arrangement of dimples in the door panel for the screws that fastened the inner works of the window and door-latch controls. (James Alexander)

A large fire extinguisher, part of the standard equipment of a wrecker, is stored on a holder on the right running board, with a clamp to steady the upper part of the apparatus. This fire extinguisher is an Alfite Model 155, manufactured by American La France Foamite Corporation of Elmira, New York. To operate it, a safety pin was pulled out of the top, the valve was opened, and the nozzle was directed at the base of the fire. (James Alexander)

A Diamond T wrecker with closed-type cab is displayed in a three-quarters front right view. The lack of a cab roof ventilator, as seen on closed-cab Diamond T 4-ton cargo trucks, is noticeable. Yellow and black caution stripes were painted on the bumpers.

The roof of the closed cab includes a pronounced V shape at its front center, to match the angle of the two windshield panels. The right windshield has been opened for ventilation purposes. The ventilator door on top of the cowl is also in the open position. (James Alexander)

The joint between the inboard and outboard panels of the front right fender is visible. The 479th Amphibious Truck Company, for which this vehicle bears replica markings, served in numerous campaigns, from North Africa to Sicily, Italy, Normandy, and Germany. (James Alexander)

This closed-cab Diamond T wrecker features a roof ventilator. This vehicle has just the stock front bumper. No markings are present. In other respects, this vehicle is similar to the closed-cab Diamond T wrecker displayed in the preceding series of photographs.

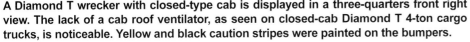

Diamond T also produced open-cab wreckers such as this example, a Model 969A. Like the Diamond T 4-ton cargo trucks, Diamond T wreckers began receiving the open-type cabs in June and July 1943. And, like the cargo versions with open cabs, the open-cab wreckers has provisions for mounting an M36 ring mount for an antiaircraft machine gun. The canvas cover, called the tarpaulin, is installed over the cab of this wrecker, and a placard with this vehicle's bridge-classification number, 12, is on the right fender.

The left light cluster consists of a service headlight, blackout marker lamp, and blackout headlight. The standard left light brush guard comprises horizontal and vertical steel wires welded to a frame, with a C-shaped extension for the blackout headlight.

The cab top and back tarpaulins are installed. On the back tarpaulin are two clear plastic windows. The two windshield panels are hinged at the top and are fitted with hold-open arms. The windshield wiper motors are faintly visible at the tops of the windshields.

Two 5-gallon liquid containers are stored in holders on the running board next to the fuel tank. Tucked into the webbing straps that retain the containers in place are collapsible watertight canvas buckets. Aft of the star is the bottom of a ring-mount bracket.

The clamp-type bracket for the steering column is visible in this view inside an open-type cab. On the left side of the dashboard is the left windshield latch; a similar one is on the right side of the cab. To the left is the glove box incorporated into the door.

CAUTION DO NOT OVERFILL
ALLOW FOR EXPANSION

A Diamond T wrecker with the open-type cab is observed from the left, showing the side profile of the tarpaulin over the cab. While all Diamond T Model 969 wreckers had closed cabs, the 969A and the export version, the 969B, were produced in both closed-cab and open-cab versions. The angle of the booms when in the stored position is apparent. The slanted or beveled front ends of the sides of the wrecker body were necessary to allow the booms to be swung to the sides.

On Diamond T wreckers, the front splash shields were bent, as shown here, with the tops of the shields fastened to the bottom of the wrecker body. At left is the left brace leg of the crane; toward the top is the yoke to which the leg is secured when not in use.

The tall cylinder is a 200-cubic-foot oxygen bottle, while the short one is a 225-cubic-foot acetylene bottle. All other oxy-acetylene welding equipment, including the torch, hoses, cutting and welding tips, and instruction book, were stored in the left body box.

In the foreground are the acetylene bottle with its retainer rod and the top of the left service drum, with the gears around the inner disc of the drum visible. In the background are the left boom, the spare tire, pioneer tools, and the end of the right boom.

The left side of the wrecker crane is viewed. Above the service drum, the bent rod through which the winch cable passes is a backlash brake loop: there is one on each side of the wrecker, and it kept the winch cable from unwinding if there was no pull on it.

The heel of the left boom and the pivoting base it is attached to are at the lower center. On the boom is part of the operating mechanism for raising and lowering the boom, including the boom-drum ratchet with a fitting for a hand crank, the pawl, and the pawl spring. Immediately below the service drum is the pinion that received power from the wrecker transmission to drive the service drum. The wrecker transmission is to the right of center, below the two upright frame members of the crane that form an inverted V.

The Model 969A was designed with two tail light assemblys, while the 969B export model had only one tail light assembly. This example has a tailgate extending the entire width of the body, as opposed to the narrow tailgate of the closed-cab wrecker seen earlier. A reflector and three steps are present on each of the rear splash shields.

The tops of two booms are seen here up close. Each boom is fitted with twin boom sheaves. The boom cable, folded over and secured into a loop with clamps, is fastened to the anchor yoke. The anchor yoke and the cable guide are secured to the sheave with a common shaft. (John Adams-Graf)

An open-cab Diamond T wrecker is seen from the rear. Stenciled in white on the tailgate is "Caution / Left / Hand / Drive," a feature commonly seen on U.S. Army vehicles that were used in the United Kingdom, where right-hand-drive vehicles were the rule. A British or Commonwealth driver mistaking a U.S. military vehicle for a right-hand-drive vehicle could have disastrous results on the narrow roads of the UK. As was typical when the booms were not in use, the hooks on the winch cables are secured to the safety rings on the cross-sill below the tailgate.

On each mast, the inboard boom sheave was meant to accommodate the boom cable, which lowered and raised the boom, while the outboard sheave was for the winch cable, which raised and lowered the load. (John Adams-Graf)

Often a spare tire was stored on the floor of the wrecker body, in addition to the spare tire on the stiff legs. Here, a spare tire is bolted to the floor, while at the top is a spare tire in its usual position. The heels of the two booms are also in view. (John Adams-Graf)

The right side of the wrecker body of a Diamond T open-cab wrecker is exhibited. A towbar is stored on its brackets on the side of the body. The recommended tire pressure for the tandem dual tires, 65 p.s.i., is stenciled in white on the wrecker body sill.

The boom cable ran from a cable drum at the heel of the boom, along the underside of the boom, over the inboard boom sheave, forward to the inboard mast sheave, and finally back to the anchor yoke at the top of the boom, where cable clamps secured it.

In this view of the right side of the crane, the boom cable is taut and it is wrapped around the inboard mast sheave. On the other hand, the winch cable is fairly slack, and it passes over the top of the outboard mast sheave on its way to the boom sheave. Yellow and black caution stripes have been painted on the towbar at the bottom of the photo.

The two upright frame members on the right side of the crane are viewed facing forward, with the back tarpaulin of the cab in the background. To the left of the central axis of the service drum is the shaft for the drum. Below it is the propeller shaft for the pinion. (John Adams-Graf)

The spare tire mounted on the stiff legs of the crane is viewed from the right rear. Both of the spotlights and mast sheaves are in view. Square-headed bolts hold the stiff legs to the mast. Steel blocks that the bolts pass through reinforce the stiff legs-mast joint.

The spotlight and the mast sheaves on the right side of the crane are viewed close-up. The taut cable running to the inboard sheave is the boom cable, which lowered and raised the boom. The cable to the right is the winch cable, the load-pulling and –lowering cable. (John Adams-Graf)

The crane on an open-cab Diamond T wrecker is observed from the right side. The chain for securing the brace leg is not wrapped around the leg but is hanging from the D-ring at the outer end of the crane. The oxygen bottle of the oxy-acetylene welding equipment is in view. The bottle rests on a holder with raised sides. Midway up the bottle, it rests against a sort of cradle, where the bottle is snugly secured by a steel rod bent in the shape of a C, which in turn is inserted through two holes in a steel plate fastened to the upright frame members. Nuts hold that rod tightly in place.

The right spotlight is viewed facing toward the rear, showing its handle, on/off switch, electrical cable, and mounting. The construction of the mast of the crane is illustrated: it comprises two channel irons with plates welded on top for the mast sheaves (left). (John Adams-Graf)

The wrecker body and part of the open-type cab are observed from the right side. A sledgehammer was part of the Diamond T wrecker's complement of tools and normally was stored in the rear toolbox, but here it has been stashed on the right boom.

This part of the right boom contained the mechanism for raising and lowering the boom and, hidden inside the boom, the boom-cable drum. The ratchet has a square fitting for attaching the operating crank, and the pawl and pawl spring are also in view.

Below the oxygen bottle holder are the right-side control levers for the winches. Controls for both winches were present are on both sides of the vehicle, with the outboard handle controlling the nearest winch and the other handle controlling the winch on the opposite side.

A wrecker transmission is observed from its right rear. This was a key component of the wrecker, as it transmitted power to the winches through propeller shafts. To the right is the right propeller shaft, shown where it passes through a fitting in the frame of the crane. (John Adams-Graf)

In a view of the front of the wrecker transmission from the right side of the vehicle, the roller chain that transmitted power from the power takeoff down below to the sprocket on the transmission is visible. The holders for the oxy-acetylene bottles also are visible. (John Adams-Graf)

The tops of the brace legs (the right one is shown to the right side of the photograph) are attached to swiveling yokes on the underside of the mast of the crane. Above the yoke is the D-ring welded to the end of the mast. On the bottom of the mast to the left of the yoke is a rubber bushing through which the winch cable passes on its way up to the mast sheave, which is visible at the top of the photo. Toward the bottom left is part of the backlash brake loop.

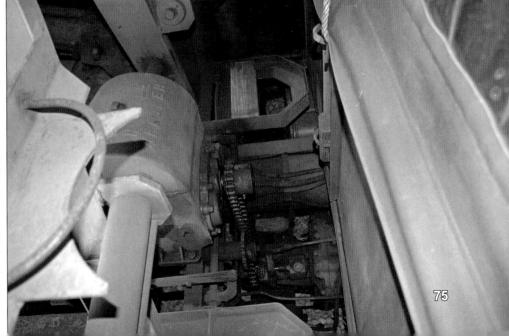

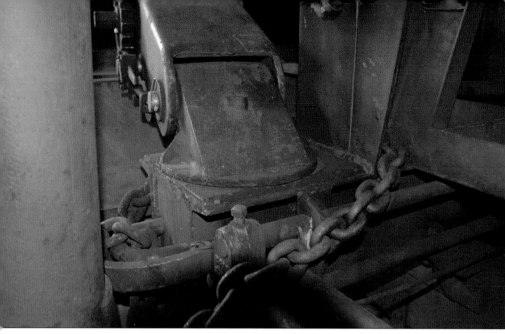

At the center of the photo is the swiveling yoke to which the heel of the right mast is fastened. This yoke allows the boom to be swung out to a right angle to the longitudinal centerline of the vehicle. A pin secures the boom to the yoke. (John Adams-Graf)

The front right corner of a Diamond T wrecker body is shown. Forward of the swiveling yoke for the right boom are the two right-side winch controls. Part of the wrecker's standard equipment was 300 feet of 1-inch-diameter rope, stored in the wrecker body.

A placard issued by the U.S. Port Agency, War Shipping Administration, New York, displaying the vehicle's weight and dimensions is painted on the door of the battery box. A carbon dioxide fire extinguisher is secured to its holder and clamp bracket.

Details of the front wheel well of a Diamond T wrecker with open cab are provided. The irons that support the fender are in view, as is the service air coupling with yellow dummy coupling to the front of the tire. To the upper left is a ring-mount bracket.

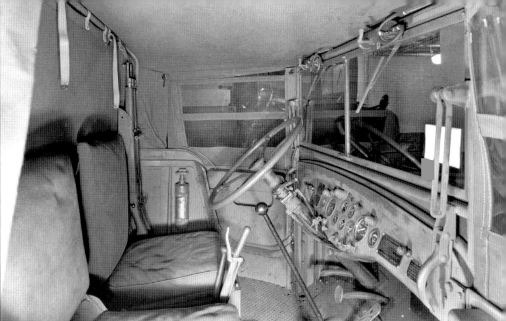

An overhead view of an open-cab Diamond T wrecker dated 1 May 1944 provides a wealth of details of the vehicle, from the ring mount for a .50-caliber machine gun over the passenger's seat to the spare tire and coil of rope on the floor of the wrecker body. (TACOM LCMC History Office)

An April 1944 photograph shows the interior of an open-cab Diamond T wrecker with the cab top tarpaulin and back tarpaulin installed. The right and left side curtains are installed. The fronts of the curtains were fastened to the sides of the windshield frame. (TACOM LCMC History Office)

The engine and accessories of a Diamond T wrecker 969A are viewed from the right side in a 3 March 1944 photograph. The arrangement of the components is similar to that displayed in the photo of an engine of a Diamond T cargo truck earlier in this book. (TACOM LCMC History Office)

This view under the hood of a Diamond T wrecker Model 969A was also taken on 3 March 1944. Prominent at the center of the photo is the oil-bath air cleaner, manufactured by the United Specialties Company. Immediately aft of it are two FRAM oil filters. (TACOM LCMC History Office)

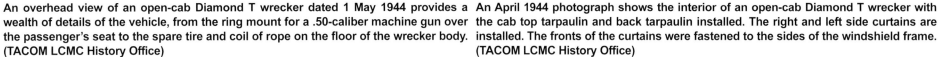

Kevin Kronlund's Diamond T wrecker with open-type cab features an immaculate Olive Drab paint scheme and plenty of markings. On the hood is a U.S. Army registration number, 4528770. The code "ASCZ 258" on the right side of the bumper stands for Advance Section, Communications Zone 258. A bridge weight classification number, 12, is on the right fender. A weight classification was carried on U.S. Army vehicles starting in 1943, and the number was based on a formula based on the vehicle's weight, size, and other factors.

A Diamond T wrecker with open-type cab is viewed from directly to the front. The bend in the center of the front bumper provided operating clearance for the cable of the front-mounted winch. The "C-23" code on the left side of the bumper stood for the 23rd vehicle in the order of march for Company C. Protruding below the bumper to the right of the star insignia is the brake housing of the winch assembly.

"Prestone 45" on the upper tank of the radiator replicates a marking used on U.S. Army vehicles in World War II meaning that antifreeze was added to the coolant system in 1945. On the windshield is a temporary shipping marking, "Ready for shipment 1/15/45."

The left service headlight, blackout headlight, blackout marker lamp, and their brush guard are the subjects of a close-up portrait. Details are also visible of the radiator and its guard, the upper radiator tank, and the louvered side panel of the hood.

The Diamond T wrecker had a net weight of 21,350 pounds and could tow another vehicle weighing up to 25,000 pounds. Whether it was the wrecker version or the various cargo and troop-carrier incarnations, the Diamond T 4-ton trucks were tough, durable, dependable, and versatile. The powerful Hercules RXC engines and all-wheel drive made them highly mobile and able to cross terrain that would foil many Axis trucks. The Diamond T 4-ton truck was a key element in keeping the U.S. armed forces well supplied and smoothly functioning, and as such, can be considered an important contributor to victory in World War II.